'BOYLE A QUART OF CREAM'

The Housekeeping Book of
Almary Greame
of Sewerby House
Bridlington
1756 – 1812

Selected and Edited
with Commentary, Notes and Decorations
by
Robin Dermond Horspool

IN AFFECTIONATE
MEMORY

DR. FRANCIS JOHNSON, CBE.
WHO ADMIRED ALMARY, KNEW AND LOVED SEWERBY HALL
LIVING FOR MANY YEARS AT LEYS HOUSE

THE EDITOR'S OWN EMPATHY WITH THE ROMANCE OF
THE PAST IS DUE, IN NO SMALL WAY, TO FRANCIS'S LONG
ASSOCIATION WITH HIM AND HIS FAMILY

British Library Cataloguing in Publication Data.
A catalogue record for this book is available from the British Library.

ISBN 1 902645 25 1

Published by

Highgate of Beverley

Highgate Publications (Beverley) Limited
4 Newbegin, Beverley, HU17 8EG. Telephone (01482) 886017

Printed by Highgate Print Limited
4 Newbegin, Beverley, HU17 8EG. Telephone (01482) 886017

CONTENTS

CONTENTS OF RECIPES

ACKNOWLEDGEMENTS

Posthumous thanks must go to my father, the late Maurice Horspool, for acquiring Almary's book in the first place and for infecting me with a similar love of it. I am also more thankful than I can say for my friendship with the late Francis Johnson, which enabled our talks on a number of joint interests, including Sewerby and Almary; it also allowed me the privilege of sitting on her dining chairs and hearing her long-case clock pass many a good-humoured hour.

I am grateful, too, to David and Susan Neave, for their initial thoughts on the possible emergence of at least some of Almary's book into the millennium's public light; my thanks go to David for his permission to include my paraphrase of David Garrick's letter from his book, *Londesborough: History of an Estate Village*.

To my research assistant in the West Riding, Juliet Horspool, go my grateful thanks for contributions which have made my labours all the more pleasurable.

To John Markham of Highgate of Beverley and Nial Adams, Principal Museum's Officer, I owe a debt of gratitude for their interest and support; as I do to Val Hill, who is getting used to transferring my work to hard disc.

I greatly value the help and advice given by my wife, Rose, particularly in those areas concerning plants and herbs; and not forgetting her ever-watchful eye on my spelling, which is known, at times, to be as colourful as Almary's.

EDITOR'S NOTE

This is a book of a book – an 18th-century collection of recipes, both culinary and medicinal. The original spelling, grammar and phraseology has been retained throughout. The only liberty has been the introduction of basic punctuation in order to help clarification of expression for the contemporary reader. A number of abbreviated words, which are little more than squiggles in the manuscript, have been written out in full for the same reason. 'Ye' in the manuscript is an old abbreviation of 'the'. The recipes are served complete and with their variations in spelling and use of Capital Letters.

AN APPETISER

With the amount of media input these days into the pleasures of the palate, there can be few remaining secrets left on the shelf. One of them, however, is surely the knack of being able to open and pour from a carton of fluid without flooding the neighbourhood. Though some manufacturers now thoughtfully provide plastic snap devices let into the cardboard, there is much work still to be done in deterring that initial blob from ejaculating like a wet cannonball onto the passing cat.

Since the television network re-opened after World War II, a veritable cornucopia of experts has served us a double menu of personality and performance: we have had seriously controlled chefs in beards and unhatted semi-baldness; Galloping Gourmets charging about with fistfuls of alcohol noisily liberating utensils; theatrical dames, backed by monocled partners, creating high living and higher cholesterol proportionate to rich working mixtures of evening dress and lordly demeanour. In their time, the Two Fat Ladies have had their scarlet fingernails in the flour bin; the personable Naked Chef has revealed his culinary charms; and mystic delights from distant creases of the Empire have been purveyed with beguiling colour and fragrance by assortments of exotic enthusiasts.

In conjunction with glossy coffee table editions of how to procure, prepare and present Everything Good To Eat and Drink, to the most minimal guide on the side of a cereal packet, there is little chance that the average individual cannot feel inspired to put the boil-in-the-bag ratatouille back in the freezer and leave the tin of fresh salmon in the cupboard. Cooking, like-gardening and transforming your living space, has never been so popular, nor so available. There is an almost bewildering array of 'do's', 'don'ts' and 'if you like's.' With so much back-up material to be found on screen and between covers hard and soft, there is little chance of the towering failures systematically encountered by Basil Fawlty and, not infrequently, Sooty and Sweep.

Back in the days before the mass media dominated home life, the presentation and enjoyment of food was looked upon as a show in itself. Time was set aside for it and it had the focus of attention the small screen has today. Much, however, could go wrong and money be wasted through lack of knowledge and even a little common sense.

Needless inadequacy and failure were the concerns of Mrs. Isabella Beeton, half-a-dozen years after the Great Exhibition of 1851. She explained that she was moved by the discomfort and suffering which she saw brought upon men and women by household mismanagement and the housewife's badly cooked dinners and untidy ways. Her help would have been invaluable, some years earlier, to the young, inexperienced David Copperfield and his new and even more inexperienced wife, Dora. Gullible in the face of unscrupulous shopkeepers and at the mercy of incompetent, dishonest servants, they typified the innocent sufferers of spoiled food, dishevelled households and raw nerves. It is debatable, though, as to how many husbands would have personally referred to the Cookery Book, as David did, to ascertain the correct length of time per pound required to roast joints. He is not too proud, however, to admit that, despite his researches, no medium could be hit on between redness and cinders.

Mrs. Beeton would also have been in sympathy with Miss Matty's devoted and plain-speaking housekeeper, Martha, in Elizabeth Gaskell's *Cranford*, published in 1853. At the time of Miss Matty's financial collapse Martha looked to food as the logical alleviator of all life's setbacks: 'I'll make her a pudding and a pudding she'll like . . . many a one has been comforted in their sorrow by seeing a good dish come upon the table.'

Isabella Mayson, aged 20 and newly married to Samuel Beeton the publisher, took four years to compile what was to become the definitive treatise on all aspects of how successfully to run a home, by covering every conceivable aspect – from the morals and philosophy of a worthy mistress of the house and her staff, through an overwhelming variety of recipes including all consumable foodstuffs. She concluded with the practicalities of rearing and managing children, their diseases, all things medical, legal and administrative. Her progressive and comprehensive treatise first began appearing in monthly parts as supplements to her husband's popular publication, *The English Woman's Domestic Magazine,* in 1859. On completion of its run, it appeared in book form under the title *Beeton's Book of Household Management,* its 1112 pages of text and evocative engravings retailing at 7 shillings and 6 pence. This was the age of the good long read; the mighty tome – *Mrs. Beeton,* as the work became affectionately known – was contemporary with Charles Dickens's *A Tale of Two Cities* and *Great Expectations*, George Eliot's *The Mill On The Floss* and *Silas Marner*. Wilkie Collins's *The Woman in White* continued to engross its audience in its net of mystery and suspense. Mrs. Beeton joined the ranks of 'best sellers'.

The reading public, avid for mental stimulation and improvement in an increasingly competitive society, thought nothing of digesting over 1700 recipes and countless morsels of homespun philosophy and advice, guaranteeing its continued publication long after the authoress's death at the age of 28, and Sam's before he was 50. Each new edition boasted it to be entirely revised, corrected and greatly enlarged, the editors honestly promising that the work was rendered complete and reliable, up-to-date and worthy of the reputation it had so long enjoyed. Along with *Cassell's Household Dictionary,* it became the bastion of knowledge and advice for the aspiring classes.

In the days before Mrs. Beeton and the Industrial Revolution, England was still almost tribal with its isolated and self-sufficient pockets of habitation away from cities and large towns. Improvements in roads and travel had yet to link them more easily, and with them a communication system which would ease the mind and body, if not sometimes, the soul. As with every age, though, the division of class was the ever-present reality which gave life its edge: the keen blade of a butcher's knife, or, as in the case of the French Revolution, scythe and guillotine.

Mrs. Beeton, also catering for mind, body and sometimes soul, is probably still one of the best known names in the history and development of the culinary arts, both of which established themselves in England during the Roman occupation. By comparison, Saxon and Viking fare relied more on substance than subtlety.

A hundred or so years after Duke William of Normandy's invasion of 1066, the English palate, as well as the language was becoming accustomed to a certain French flavour and the writing down of hints and recipes, the first important treatise being by the Augustian canon Alexander Neckham, later Abbot of Cirencester.

Six hundred years and many works further on, from *The Forme of Cury* (Cookery) dedicated to Richard II, through *The Good Huswives Closet* of 1591 and John Murrell's *Two Books of Cookerie and Carving* of 1638, to Patrick Lamb's *The Compleat Court Cook* of 1710, the 18th century produced the largest selection to date. The publications were wide-ranging, many of them now supplied by women, of whom Hannah Glasse and Elizabeth Raffald remain pioneers, establishing the English tradition which Mrs. Beeton was to reinforce in the next century.

By 1817, when Joseph Bell brought out his *Treatise On Confectionary,* the Prince Regent, later George IV, was benefiting from the services of Antonin Carême, one time chef to Napoleon Bonaparte. The Prince was also known as the First Gentleman of Europe, not least for his appreciation of French cuisine. At Carlton House and under the copper palm leaves in the Marine Pavilion's kitchen at Brighton, Carême enjoyed a free hand, also writing several of his own books. Dedicated to his art, he thought nothing of having to supply over a hundred separate dishes for a single banquet in January, 1817, justly earning his annual salary of £2,000.

Other suppliers of royal insight were also weighing out from their personal garners, for in 1845, Eliza Acton in her *Modern Cookery for Private Families* was able to quote a recipe entitled The Regent's Punch (see Appendix II), the provenance of which she then felt it her personal responsibility to verify: We are indebted for this receipt *(sic)* to a person who made this punch daily for the Prince's table, at Carlton House Palace, for six months; it has been in our possession some years and may be relied on. Eliza Acton, amongst others, was also the unacknowledged inspiration for much of Isabella Beeton's material but lacked the promotional qualities Samuel brought to his wife's labours and reputation he traded on after her death.

Soyer, Francatelli and Ranieri added to increasingly cosmopolitan preferences, with Escoffier, one of the great names to bridge the 19th and 20th centuries, sharing his craft in *A Guide to Modern Cookery.*

THE GREAMES TAKE STOCK

Back in the mid 18th century, then, the wealth of printed matter available contributed favourably to the aspirations of the affluent classes which were forming the backbone of the Age of Enlightenment. It was also the Age of the Country House and Huge Staff Needed to Run It. The Grand Tour was obligatory for even a cursory brush with the roots of educated civilisation – including, if possible, the purchase or purloinment of at least one piece of antique statuary. The necessity of one's association with classical ideals was likely to facilitate social acceptance, an event succinctly distilled by Dr. Johnson when he observed that a man who had not been to Italy was conscious of an inferiority, almost all that sets us above the savages having come from the shores of the Mediterranean.

Not least amongst the concerns of those wealthy patrons employing Mr. Adam and Mr. Holland to modernise their old fashioned properties or design new ones, were the departments connected with the preparing, cooking, serving, consuming and clearing of food and drink. No longer did the servants live and interact with the family on an equal basis as they had done in medieval times. Safety in numbers, in case of attack or invasion by the enemy without, was no longer a priority, the role and status of servants and retainers becoming relegated to behind-the-scenes presences – rarely seen, never heard. They had their own quarters and working spaces and were expected to 'know their place.'

The Country House Style was established, food being one of the major features by which to measure the Good Life: to see and be seen – to host and be hosted. No opportunity was lost for assembled humanity with any crumb of aspiration (and not a few crumbs of finance) to parade and dally in finest apple green silks and crushed rose brocades; to exchange pleasantries and witticisms, gossip and scandal; even to wax intellectual, political, lyrical or romantic amongst the restrained opulence of Neo-Classical eating rooms, whose clustered candles branching in all directions, illumined polished surfaces: sheen of mahogany and marble flooded with silver, silver-gilt, glass; with porcelain bearing all manner of savouries and sweetmeats mirrored in endless pier glasses lustrous with showers of cut crystal drops spangling the gilded spaces.

Along with contemporary country gentlemen, such were the aspirations of John Greame the Younger when he inherited Sewerby House and its lands on his father's death in 1746. A 37-year-old bachelor with a love of horses, he found himself comfortably provided for, thanks to his father's two financially advantageous marriages. His father had also enjoyed a further boost from his bay horse, Champion, which had won Queen Anne's Gold Cup at the York Races in 1713. John Greame the Elder had first leased, then purchased, the Sewerby estate, finding the Manor House to be an out-dated and inconvenient hotch-potch progressively altered with little or no cohesion.

What John Greame the Younger contemplated in 1746 was his father's rebuilding of 1714-20: an early Neo-Classical essay with Baroque undertones in line with the fashionable inventions of William Kent, born in the High Street of nearby Bridlington Old Town. Though never working at Sewerby, Kent and his patron Richard Boyle, 3rd Earl of Burlington, had continued to anglicise the Italian style adapted earlier by Inigo Jones and Christopher Wren. But the new Sewerby House was no St. Paul's Cathedral, nor fanciful extravaganzas like John Vanbrugh's Castle Howard or Blenheim Palace. John Greame's practical elegance formed a simple, even severe, block of three storeys and seven bays, box-like in handmade red brick with stone dressings, parapet surmounted with central pediment, arch-topped window above a front door with fanlight unencumbered by portico or *porte-cochere*. The cliff top site swept across to the abrupt edge, where the German Ocean took over, stretching the eye; there was the view, arcing round to the flash of chalk headland at Flamborough on the left, and Burlington Quay away on the right, before asserting itself on a taut horizon shelving a high-piled skyscape.

His father's house faced this vista with assurance: how well in the southward sun the soft warm-hued brickwork glowed on its open swathes of verdure edged by the sea, like a good tomato in a bed of lettuce on a blue plate. The rather isolated house, amongst its open plains of communal village fields, was to become more protected and private after the Enclosure Acts; the landscaping of the grounds and the planting of banks of trees developed once parts of old Sewerby village and fields had been reallocated in the early 19th century. But in the 1740s, John's father had owned a simple and honest environment, with a house of gentle dignity mellowing in long summer suns and defying brusque winter onslaughts blasting across from Scandinavia, Siberia and the Arctic.

John might have recalled that, when the Duke of Buckingham had fashioned for himself a new London mansion at the west end of St. James's Park 40 or so years earlier, he, too, had delighted in its distinguished position. As it commanded an impressive catchment from Westminster to the City and St. Paul's, via a broad-flowing Thames, Buckingham had advertised his joy by emblazoning, in gilded Latin, the frieze above the central pilasters of the east front with the inscription: *SIC SITU LAETANTUR LARES* – The Household Gods delight in such a situation. John, though lacking the Duke's ostentation and even more ostentatious wife, might well have felt similarly inclined. He resisted, however, perhaps being aware that his family motto: *C'EST LA SEULE VERTU QUI DONNE LA NOBLESSE* – It is virtue alone which gives nobility – had a subtlety about it sufficient to enable the house to become a manifestation of the noble virtue contained within. Coupled with the house's obviously noble situation, here were two sentiments vital to the appreciation of any *locus amenus*★ or *genius loci*★★

For a further 10 years, John remained a bachelor living with his mother in his pavilion-by-the-sea, with its carved woodwork and unpainted panelling, its pilasters and decorative mouldings; it was still very much his father's house in concept and atmosphere. Then, in 1756, he brought to it his new bride, the lady who was to see in the onset of the Industrial Revolution.

Alicia Maria Spencer of Cannon Hall, Cawthorne, near Barnsley, was 33-years-old when she became the new Mistress of Sewerby. Her father had died the same year, his estates passing to his eldest son, John. Five years Alicia's senior, he remained unmarried. Their sister Anne, wife of Walter Stanhope, provided the son, Walter, who was to inherit his Uncle John's property in 1775, when he prefixed his own surname with Spencer. As Walter Spencer-

★place of delight
★★guardian spirit of a place

Stanhope, he became one of the family recipients of his Aunt Alicia's correspondence once she had become established on the East Coast of Yorkshire, where she was known in family circles as Almary.

Her other sister, Christina Shuttleworth, also acted as a focus for literary communication, for, with poor or non-existent roads linking the Ridings across the Wolds, frequent letters were more likely than visits. Almary savoured the minutiae of everyday life which, as far as she was concerned, was a peaceful, happy existence with her husband amongst the kindly contours of their cliff-top prominence.

One can imagine Almary taking her duties seriously; being Mistress of a Country House was not dissimilar, in modern terms, to being the Manageress of a five star hotel. She would have had to possess a natural expectation of quality, value for money, fair and honest dealing, with an inability to suffer fools gladly. Though the east coast of the East Riding was not exactly in the white heat of London competition, she was keen to be kept abreast of current fashions, news and gossip, being most particular in ordering new furnishings for the house. This was often through her brother, John, back at Cannon Hall, an establishment not unlike Sewerby in date, materials and appearance. She trusted his taste implicitly, which she described as 'fine,' agreeing with her sister Stanhope that she would not buy by any other person's fancy. She acquired several tables, sets of chairs, exuberant rococo mirrors in the latest French style, a black and gold Chinese lacquered long case clock by Samuel Atkinson, the local supplier of excellence; and a dozen mahogany dining chairs in the Chippendale style made by a Wakefield firm as a composite design from *The Gentleman's and Cabinet Maker's Director* of 1754.

ALMARY WHETS THE APPETITE

It was this desire to be in fashion and in control, as well as a natural pleasure in the task, which may well have led to the compilation of her Household Book. She was also following the tradition of many of her contemporaries whose main objectives were to help freshly married ladies to be mistresses of well-run households.

With a reliable housekeeper, this was easier to achieve, but housekeepers had to be trained, and an intelligent and sympathetic mistress was essential not only to maintain standards but also to retain staff, thus earning a good reputation amongst her social equals; reliable and loyal staff being at a premium, these were not to be lost lightly. The household could be looked upon as the Factory of Life, having to be self-sufficient and to provide virtually everything an enhanced survival relied on, to the making of soap, ink, candles, bread, butter, cheese, with meals planned using seasonal produce: fish, meat and game shot and caught on the estate, fruit and vegetables grown in the gardens; and good local grocers providing luxury commodities such as loaf sugar, dried fruits and spices. Drinking water could be of dubious origin in many instances, so there was a good deal of home brewing, with a variety of beers and wines, particularly when the house was full of guests.

Almary's and John's marriage remained childless, so their household did not have to be large – Almary found that she could oversee its management with an inborn aptitude and pride which encouraged her to foster the reputation of not seeming provincial. In addition to her own astute observations with which she constantly filled her correspondence, she would avail herself of the printed word, if need be. As a modern home manager, she could well have come across Nicolas Chomel's *Family Dictionary* of 1725 and Richard Bradley's *Country Housewife and Lady's Director* of 1727, both dealing with pursuits relating to the house and its garden. 1730, seven years after her birth, had also seen the popularity of Eliza Smith's *The Compleat Housewife or Accomplished Gentlewoman's Companion,* which considered cookery and issues relating to the kitchen. These areas were more thoroughly covered in *The Art of Cookery made Plain and Easy*, one of the great domestic books of the age, brought out in 1747 by 'A Lady' – better known as Mrs. Hannah Glasse, who went on to bring out *The Servant's Directory or Housekeeper's Companion* 13 years later. Over 300 works concerning cookery and food appeared between 1700 and 1800, many of them going into several editions.

Much of the standard recipes would necessarily have had to be adapted to the household's circumstances or availability of ingredients, depending on location and time of year. Cooks were encouraged to be resourceful and inventive when occasion demanded. To this end, Edward Kidder brought out his *Receipts of Pastry and Cookery for the Use of his Scholars.* The title page informs readers that he teaches at his school in St. Martin's-le-Grand on Mondays, Tuesdays and Wednesdays in the afternoon, and also on Thursdays, Fridays and Saturdays in the afternoon at his school next to Furnival's Inn, Holborn. 'Ladies,' he adds obligingly, 'may be taught at their own houses.'

Six years before Almary's marriage, William Ellis's *Country Housewife's Family Companion* made the point of combining what was concocted in the kitchen with what was concocted by the apothecary to alleviate its periodic results. For centuries, food and physic had shared equal status, and no self-respecting mistress of any house could afford to be ignorant of basic health and medical matters. Except for specific complaints, there tended to be a grey area of ill-health which generally related to the stomach, digestive system and thus the 'humour' of the body. This was hardly surprising considering the amount of food consumed, which was liable to be not in its prime and probably cooked with variable proficiency in not always hygienic conditions. Diets tended also to be low on basic fresh vegetables which, though grown in the gardens, helped bulk out the servants' diets. They aspired to higher consumption when drenched in sauces, or, if they were exotic, like mushrooms, broccoli and asparagus.

For thousands of years, the use of plants and herbs had continued to provide a large proportion of remedies which were intended to lessen discomfort or pain. For mortal ailments, if they were recognised and understood, surgery was the extreme outpost which, until the middle of the 19th century, was carried out without the benefits of anaesthetics, other than generous intakes of brandy – a commodity also figuring generously in many a recipe or receipt, as it was known. Numbers of these were handed down from generation to generation, with modifications and improvements added along the way, sometimes including notes on personal experience.

Good health was taken seriously and prized in an age of elegance stained with high mortality and not a long life expectancy. Coupled with an incomplete understanding of hygiene-related issues, there was also no regulation of drug and medicine usage – no awareness of what we would nowadays term 'dangerous drugs.' For ready money a sympathetic apothecary would supply anything the customer requested, whether suitable or not, the majority of ailments and their cures being attended to within the household. The editor's mother-in-law well remembers, as a young child growing up in a rural part of Co. Kildare, Eire, accidentally biting her tongue nearly clean through and suffering acute agony. With no telephone nor car available, though it was the early 1930s, her elderly guardian went round the kitchen scooping up cobwebs like candy floss and bandaging the injury with them. After 24 hours' rest in bed 'and no talking,' she was allowed up, her tongue greatly healed, and being Easter, no impediment to the enjoyment of a chocolate egg. Doctors' expenses were reserved for major disasters, epidemics and death, of which there was no shortage, particularly amongst the young – John Greame the Younger was, himself, one of the few survivors of his parents' 12 children.

At Castle Howard is still preserved the handwritten volume belonging to Isabella, 4th Countess of Carlisle, emphatically entitled *My Book of Receipts,* a collection of gastronomic indulgences and medicinal cures. Viscount Fairfax in Castlegate, York, and at Gilling Castle, had a household book kept – a transcribed mixture of apothecary's shop and cook's kitchen, many of the recipes deriving from Hannah Glasse and Eliza Smith. But unlike the *Arcana Fairfaxiana Manuscripta*, Almary's book has no title but fits into the Carlisle/Fairfax category. She was not concerned with compiling yet another instructional treatise on servant and household management, but simply a personal collection, as was the fashion. There was a good chance that like many other books commenced at the time or in a process of continuation, hers would be added to by future generations, building it into an invaluable boiling pot of information and experience. Her family were aware of her interest and kept her supplied with items they thought would interest her or for which she asked.

Her book measures 13 inches by 8 inches (33 cm x 20 cm) and contains 150 pages of medium duty cream paper. When opened out, each sheet, folded in the centre, bears on the left-hand page the watermark of a crown with G.R. beneath, signifying King George II. On the right-hand side, a coroneted lion brandishing a scimitar and sheaf of arrows does his best to look fierce within a circular fence on which a helmeted Britannia diplomatically sits. From a gate at the front hangs a bell bearing the letter J, with above the design the legend, *Pro Patria* – 'For One's Country'. The pages are cut and clean-trimmed, bound between tooled tan-leather-covered cards and stitched into the spine.

It is divided into two sections. One way up, the main bulk contains over 550 recipes and advice alphabetically indexed and page numbered, from 'Apricock Briskett' to 'Syllabub Cheese'; flipped over and the other way up, an equally thorough index opens a pharmacopoeia under the heading 'Various Medcins'. It contains nearly 180 compounds and cures, from Ague to Worms. Judging by the wear on this side of the cover, the remedies have been more often consulted than the recipes, many of which acknowledge the donor.

The pages are written in a number of differing hands, a goodly portion of which are in Almary's. They contain several styles of copperplate, some more flourishing than others, penned in sepia ink from the ends of cut quills, some sharper and finer than others. Almary's is fairly coarse and her handwriting firmer and less fanciful, with a minimum of curvilinear decoration, as though writing as scrolly as a rococo handrail got in the way of 'making a proper job of it', as they say in Yorkshire. It could be that she either inherited the beginnings of this book from her mother or that her mother or a relative began it for her prior to her duties as a married woman. The earlier entries are in a more old fashioned hand inscribed with the degree of controlled flourish to be seen on engravers' plates. Further research could, indeed, reveal that the book may have been handed on to her by her mother-in-law. With Almary continuing what had been started, other hands suggest that they also used the book rather like an autograph album for friends to inscribe a culinary contribution. In some instances, they have written their own names or have had them added later by Almary.

There are many touching little insights into the human process of creation: 'boyle (the sugar) till it come to Candy height', or 'heat till new milk warm'. Particularly graphic is 'beat your Cake well with your Hand an Hour'. If you are not too exhausted by February, you are advised that then is the best time for brewing strong beer but that it will be two years before you can drink it. Some of the recipes contain personal notes: we are told that Betty always puts the pancakes on a dish cover because it helps her to make them lie more evenly; Almary's sister remarks that for her Mighty Plum Cake she uses only a quarter of the ingredients; in Mrs. Washington's opinion, raisins from Smyrna make the best wine.

Many of the recipes seem to rely on using ingredients already made up from other recipes, such as the use of forcemeat, which is included singly and as an integral ingredient. Recipes and working methods can also be remarkably vague, as though having a natural reliance on some sort of fore-knowledge on the part of the cook or reader, signifying complete accord between like-minded persons. This is true, too, of the medical concerns, with the composition of the compounds given but sometimes not what ailments they are for. Occasionally, quite bizarre images are unintentionally invoked: 'batter your papers', and 'lay your ears in the middle'. Most eye-watering of all is the direction to 'skin your sweetbreads'.

The contents cover a wide range of tips and processes, from the straightforward cooking of meats and fish to the making of savouries, breads, cakes, biscuits, tarts and sweets; there is the candying of flowers, preservation of fruit, and the making of sauces, wines, sack and mead.

It can be difficult today to appreciate the complete lack of all the advantages we take for granted: refrigeration, detergents, running water, instantly controllable heat and labour-saving devices which do not smoke, steam or smell, even if they do crash, bang and whirr. There was an absence, too, of the commercial provision of basic commodities and ingredients; households such as Almary's had, in proportion to their needs, to be self-sufficient in rearing, fattening, growing, churning, distilling, cooking and disposing. With the sometimes dubious age and condition of some meats, herbs were used in abundance to disguise and enhance questionable flavours. These could be grown in a suitable plot of the kitchen garden. There were town and village markets, but it was the estate, first and foremost, which was looked to for well husbanded produce. By the end of the 18th century, the English upper classes had made this particularly their own and it is this legacy which pervades the wider social class structure of the 19th, since when it has become tradition.

One of the particular pleasures of the recipes' style is the human and personal involvement at every level, addressed by the writers, as if they are speaking directly to those taking part in the sometimes lengthy and complex processes required. There is continual reference to 'your pigg' and 'your tarts', and bottled ketchup or syrup of violets is to be kept for 'your use'. The processes also manage to convey a slower passing of time and quieter pace of life, nowhere more evident than in directions for making Orange Tarts:

> Take your Oranges and Rasp them, then put them into water 2 or 3 days, Shifting them once a day. Then take out ye juice and boyle them tender then take them and Cutt them. Putt to them near their Weight in Sugar. Boyle them well together then put in the juice into your Tarts.

A jar of Tesco's marmalade might have to do just as well nowadays, but a three day span on an occasional delicacy was not considered out of the way for those used to creating everything from scratch. Reading the recipe, one assumes that Cook already knew how to make the actual tarts to hold this citric invasion.

There are instances of startlingly vivid action: after the Burnt Cream has set thick in the dish and topped with sugar, there is the direction to have a hot fire shovel ready to hold over the top to brown it.

The kitchen fires alone, from quick to slow, needed constant regulation for baking, boiling, poaching, broiling, roasting and fuelling warming pans; English Country Houses were not renowned for their warmth and the Greames' exposed east coast dwelling, however fine the inside, would probably never be regarded as cosy.

Almary's book is obviously the product of a cultivated family keen to maintain its improved financial and social status. Many of the dishes contain specific ingredients: Seville oranges, Jamaican pepper, Smyrna raisins, Rhenish wine. The occasional inclusion of French ideas is also an indication of a wider appreciation; one can almost sense the delicacy and finesse with which the French recipe for preserving peaches is phrased and laid on the page, like the tender putting to bed of a young child. A knowledge of Latin is useful, for in Burnt Cream is a reference to the use of laurel. This is the *Laurus nobilis,* better known in English as sweet bay, and not to be confused with *Prunus laurocerasus,* the common laurel – one could not afford to be an ignorant mistress nor a careless cook. If the worst *did* come to the worst, then there was always the pharmacopoeia within hurried page-flicking distance.

In marked contrast was the harsher work-a-day world outside the park gates where a third of the population were estimated to be living on the threshold of starvation. Here, too, the tenant farmer, the countryman and the labourer were working land which, in many cases, was helping to provide even greater wealth for its owners in their big houses.

The workers' days were long and hard – pared down to basic necessities – their dwellings and way of life reflecting a realistic approach to practicalities, minimal incomes saving them from the tedious stress of constantly fleeting fashions. Here the Derby porcelain found its counterpart in roughly glazed earthenware little changed since the Romans; the patina of homely pewter stood in for the glint of gilt and silver; and a walk-in, sit-in yeoman kitchen fireplace clanking with a few hanging cauldrons formed the very heart of the single main living – eating – often sleeping-room.

The scrubbed deal table invites partakers to simple food with no choice of courses. Unless excused by extreme poverty, it is usually provided three times a day, the main meal acting as the welcome comfort-stop after many hours of outside toil. Fresh from the ladle comes a dish of pork or bacon stew (perhaps beef or mutton on Saturdays), or a concoction from entrails and offal such as tripe, faggots or haggis; locally shot pigeons or blackbirds make up well into pies, sparrows proving more difficult as about 30 are needed to equal a good pound of meat. There are potatoes and green vegetables often cooked into seasonal stews and soups, A regional Yorkshire pudding doused in rich stew gravy works out cheaply, and, like Norfolk dumplings, is good and filling.

Also filling is the home-baked bread, dark and coarse with rye, oats or barley, and well slabbed with cheese, butter or lard. In common with others living by the sea, there may be the opportunity for smoked or pickled herrings, and though fish is generally costly, it is possible to run to pickled sprats, oysters and even salmon now and then. Whereas those at the Big House could well be dining every day on all manner of fish regardless of expense, smoked or salted haddock might be looked on as an annual treat.

Beer, cider and milk make the standard mouth-wash with which to swill down these substantial intakes. Equally substantial sleep closes these bodily and gastronomical activities until cock-crow announces a plain breakfast of oatmeal porridge and continuing labours. This is what the granary of life has been garnering since about the age of eight. It will, during sowing, hay-making and harvest, last from early dawn to late dusk and circle its yearly round until physical energy, health or life runs out.

What a world away all this is from a guest of Robert Walpole's at Houghton Hall who wrote that he was one of a snug little party of about 30, up to the chin in beef, venison, geese, turkeys, etc. and generally over the chin in claret, strong beer and punch. Considering that Walpole spent £15 a night on the finest beeswax candles with which to illuminate Houghton for his guests, (the average labouring wages was about 12 shillings a week at harvest time and 5 shillings during the winter – 20 shillings making up the pound), he puts the countryman in the shade, lit only by a fitful tallow dip or two or smoking rushlight. Both were quickly burnt and reeked of animal fat.

Such are the ingredients of social disparity – the dish of the day throughout the preceding and succeeding generations.

A HANDFUL OF TIME

So. You have been conducted over the house and lands by your genial host and hostess; you have commented politely on the success of the improvements to the estate; on the fine appointment of the stocky mansion; on the choice of this painting and that fabric. You are now directed into the oak panelled dining room on the right of the entrance hall, to drink in the well-favoured sight before you: the fluted Corinthian pilasters modelled as crisply as a good pie crust; at the foot of the shell-headed apse in the left hand wall, a nest of ice in a lead-lined cistern, from the top of which protrude the necks of dumpy green bottles – as if they are songbirds, ready to pour forth liquid music into clusters of long-stemmed wine glasses; behind the door, a buffet steadying itself beneath a responsibility of plate, food and fine attractions; on the right-hand wall, a pair of window embrasures squaring the Arcadian view across refreshing grass and fields to the flashing waters of the German Ocean reflecting a cloudscape as white as the ceiling and damask cloth drifting the oblong table.

Here are some of Almary's newly acquired Chippendale chairs, the rest backed against the walls round the room, as this is not a vast banquet but a serene gathering of chosen friends and a pair of Spencer relations, all of whom, nevertheless, expect to be and will be discreetly impressed. You well know that hospitality, and particularly power and wealth, are best displayed at table, with an overloading of foods, monogrammed porcelain and silver; as much use of that expensive commodity – sugar – is an advisable ingredient also. Was it Shakespeare who said that you could always distinguish a gentleman by the condition of his teeth? The Chinese lacquer longcase clock in the hall chimes four in the afternoon, the signal for you to take your seat before your well furnished place setting of silver, china and glass, with a warm roll keeping its heat under the fold of your smooth linen napkin. The spoons and forks are turned face downwards so that they are less likely to catch in the flood of lace frothing at your wrists. Round you, the stockade of colours, shapes, textures and fragrances mingle with seasonal flowers and greenery softening the harder edges of the sumptuous space.

There are more than a dozen choices presented for the first course, but, as you are aware, of the 30 or so dishes available over the entire meal, you are not expected to bloat yourself with everything. This entitles you to discount immediately the Calves Head Pye, the Cream Curds and the Fricasey of Mushrooms, preferring the Beef Soop, Pickl'd Salmon and the Smelts Dissolved Like Anchovies, with perhaps a garnish of Beef and Clarett Ketchop because you simply cannot resist.

The second course is more problematic. You know how fond you are of well larded meats and you love Stewed Rump of Beef, also Pigg Pye. The Ragoo of Sweetbreads sounds interesting and there are some Coller Eells. But you have already had fish, so you decide on the Beef and the Pigg and some Forced Meat Balls and Hogs Feet and Ears. You are not sure what Puddings of Pigg Blood are and feel disinclined to find out.

With the appearance of the third course, a certain hesitancy seems to make choices slower. Peaches in Brandy might be refreshing. Spanish Licquorice? Merangues? Lemon Cream? But just look at that silver filigree èpergne groaning like Atlas beneath the world under its bobbly pyramid of Manus Christi – who ever thought of covering sugar paste marbles in gold leaf? What a sweet way of gilding the gingerbread! Rinsing your sticky fingers yet again in your crystal water bowl, you decide you will most likely have a smear of everything, not forgetting the Candied Fruits, Marchpanes, Mackroons, Jellies and Blancmanges. The London Wiggs look most acceptable too – and the Burnt Cream.

You have not been unaware, neither, of your intake of some appealing fluids: sherries and ports, champagnes and a variety of wines, peppery and sweet – the amber whites and ruby reds now having gained an added lustre with the lighting of the candles in their gleaming silver sconces; for the meal and conversation, enhanced by the silent efficiency of serving footmen, has taken several hours and dusk is beginning to roll apace across the Elysian Fields. The ladies are about to withdraw to their tea and tittle-tattle in the panelled room across the hall; there is the silver tray on its tripod table inviting attendance as welcoming as an open hand before a fire, with its array of delicate little Chelsea bowls in deep saucers, the spirit kettle comfortably steaming within easy reach.

The gentlemen remain behind, left to their port and politics; the cloth is removed in order to reveal a mirror-like expanse of finely figured mahogany reflecting decanters, glasses and comports of fruits and biscuits. Several reliefs of nature into discreet but immediate chamber pots will be passed before the world and its problems are put to rights. Then the ladies will be joined for some hands of whist or *vingt-et-un* beneath the flares of candle flame sentinel in the close summer air.

With the distant hope that breakfast is a long time away, you trace measured steps quietly to the privacy of your guest chamber where you seek out the glass-stoppered bottle of mixture you brought from home, made up from the small manuscript folio you yourself are compiling:

FOR AN INDIGESTION

Infuse a Qr. of an ounce of ye best Rhubarb in half a pint of
Double distilled Anniseed Water. Let is stand two days and it is
fit for use. It is not to be strained off. Two teaspoonfuls must be
taken every day Immediately after Dinner. Avoid Malt Liquor,
drink Mint-tea and now and then eat a Toast in red wine with
sugar and nutmeg. If it should continue, wash your Stomach
with Chamomile Tea.

On the retirement of her guests, Almary will doubtless congratulate herself
on a successful outcome to her planning – perhaps she will visit the
subterranean kitchen in the morning to suggest to Cook that, when Burnt
Cream is next served, the sugar topping will need to be browner. In the
meantime, she wishes to complete one outstanding task before retiring.
Opening her book on the bureau and taking up her quill, she shakes back her
lace cuffs and begins transcribing a new possibility recently received from a
mellifluent friend:

TO MAKE ALMOND PUDDING

Boyle a quart of Cream with Mace and Cynamand, then strain
it and thicken it with White Bread Crumbs and ½ of Almonds
very small beaten, Ye Yolks of 8 Eggs and the Whites of 4. Season
it with Nuttmeg and Sugar and let the Cloth you Boyle it in be
very well Buttered. It will take half an hours boyling.

'Yes, that will do very well for next time.' Looking forward to the following
day's post, which could contain letters from Lady Foulis or Mrs. Hodgson of
Buxton with exciting new enclosures, Almary leaves her book open to dry
and goes upstairs to join her husband, who is already snoring.

Should you have made a remarkable recovery in the night, you may feel
disposed to take up your flat candlestick and venture downstairs in search of
your hostess's account of the delicacies you ingested, if not completely
digested. Almary has made no secret of her interest in providing a good table
and you know where she keeps her book, having been shown it earlier. You
descend the staircase and by the light of the flickering flame, as the moonlit
sea rakes the beach below, you begin a systematic perusal of the recently
consumed menu . . .

HOW TO MAKE A CALVES HEAD PYE

Take two Calves Heads and cleanse them from the Blood and parboyle them. Cut them in thin Slices from the Bone and cutt your Tounge in thin slices, then season your meat with Nutmegs, Cloves, Mace, pepper and Salt and some Savoury herb finely Shread or dryed. 5 or 6 Anchovies nipt into Little bitts and thrown into your meat.

Then make some Savoury Balls,[1] take either Veal or Mutton to one part of your meat and two parts of Beef Suit finely shred. Then season your meat with Nutmeg, Mace, Cloves, pepper, salt and a little Lemon Pile[2] finely shred. Mix to it 2 Raw Eggs, a little old Bread Grated. Mix all these together and make them into long and Round Bales, then make up your Pye.

Lay the bottom of your Dish Buttery, lay on the Top of the Meats with Butter, some Slices of Lemon and whole pickled Oysters, then lay on other meats, then lay on Butter, then lay on Oysters and Lemon and Balls and 7 or 8 whole Egg Yolks boyled hard. In the middle of your Pye put an Onyon.

Cover the top of it with Butter and so close it up at the Oven Mouth. Have ready a Gill of Claret, some strong broth and half a pound of Butter. Boyle in it an Anchovie and an Onyon, then take your Onyon out then Cutt up your Pye and pour in the Gravey and so serve it up but be sure to take out the Onyon in the middle.

TO CREAM CURDS

Take three pints of New Milk, three pints of Water, set it on a Quick Fire. Take a quart of Sweet Cream, a pint of Sower Cream, Six Eggs well beat. Mix your Cream and Eggs well together.

Put it in when you see your Milk begin to Rise with a Scin. Lay 'em on a cloth upon a Sive. When they're Drained, hang 'em up in a fine Cloth a little time.

FRICASEY OF MUSHROOMS

Take your Mushrooms and wash 'em, boyle 'em in Milk and Water and Salt and a little Mace and a few sweet herbs. Thicken it with ye yolks of Eggs, a little Cream with Nutmeg grate. Take out your Herbs and Mace before you thicken 'em.

BEEF SOOP

Take a leg of Beef and set it on over night with 4 Quarts of Water, and good Bunch of sweet herbs, 2 or 3 Onions, Cloves and pepper, then Strain it the next morning and scum the fatt of. Put in the stew pan and grate on it some French Bread, putting in One Slice of Lemon Pile and one or two Anchovies. Cutt 3 or 4 Slices of Lean fresh Beef and fry them brown in a frying pan. Take 'em out and drain 'em from the Butter. Put them in the stew pan to the broth and Let it boyle a little while. Then take the Beef and Lemon Pile out, fry some good forced balls and put in and some fryed Bread. Roast a Duck and put in with the Belley downwards, or a French Loaf whole in stead of ye Duck.

TO PICKLE SALMON

Take a Salmon of 15lbs. Wipe it very clean, take out ye Gutts and Gills. When you wipe it you will see some small Veins in ye side. Force out ye Blood then wipe it clean. Cut your Salmon in four streight overcross. Take half an ounce of Black Pepper and near a Pinch of Salt. Mix them together and Season your Salmon. Put it into a pott and set it till next day, then Tye it up in Bags like Sturgeon.

Take 2 quarts of Alegar,[3] 3 quarts of water, a good deal of bay leaves, 20 or 30 half Ounce of whole pepper, a little more Salt, six pennyworth of Mace and 6 of Cloves. Put it into a Kettle.[4] When it boyles, put in your Salmon and your brine that ran from it. Half an hour will boyle it. Take it up when Cold. Put it up and keep it for Use. You may add or diminish according to the Bigness of your Salmon.

TO MAKE SMELTS[5] DISSOLVE LIKE ANCHOVIES

Take 60 Smelts, gutt them at the Gills and wipe them with a Cloth. Then Salt them with Salts peeter[6] and Bay Salt till they be Red. Then buy one pound of Anchovies and get as much of the pickle with it as you can, and then boyle them in their own pickle till they be dissolved and then let it stand till it be cold. Then pour it on your Smilts – cover them close and keep them for your use. They must be Salmon Smilts.

BEEF AND CLARETT KETCHOP

Take 3 quarts of Beef Brine that is very sweet. Put it to a quart of Clarett, 6 or 8 Anchovies, half a pint of the juice of mushrooms, 6oz of whole pepper and a few cloves. Boyle them all together in a pan and Clarifye it with roach-allum[7] about the Bigness of an Egg beaten very fine. Then strain it through a Hair Seive and when it is Cold, bottle it up for your use.

Second Course

TO STEW A RUMP OF BEEF

Powder it 2 or 3 days then stuff it well with Beef suit, grated bread and a Little sweet marjoram and time, a good handfull of parsley and some oysters, one or two onions, some Nutmeg and Mace beaten and a little Salt. Work all together with the Yolks of 2 Eggs, boyle it 4 Hours then take it up and Stew it Half an Hour in as much of the Liquor as will cover it. Put in the Rhind of half a Lemon, a little whole pepper, 2 or 3 Blades of Mace, an Onion Stuck with Cloves, half a pint of white wine, and when it is half stewed, take a pint of the liquor and in fuse 2 Anchovies in it. Then put in a Glass of white wine and good quantity of Capers and pickled Cockles shred small, also pickled Oysters and mushrooms, 2 Hard Eggs and some grated Bread. Stew all these together till they be Ready, then shake in a Lump of Butter and pouer on the Beef. Garnish it with Orange, Lemon and Barberries.[8]

TO MAKE A PIGG PYE

Take the 4 Quarters of a good Pigg and par boyle them, then take ye Skin Clear of and cutt them in Slices the length of your little finger. Season it with a little salt, ginger, mace and some Cloves and a Nutmeg and some sweet Herbs and Sage. Pinch the herbs very small and put these into the Dish or Coffin with as much Butter as you think fit. Take some white wine and the Yolks of three eggs. Make a cawdle[9] of it and put it in the pye when it comes out of the Oven.

A RAGOO OF SWEETBREADS

Take your sweet breads and Skin 'em. Put some Butter in your Frying pan and brown it with Flower. Put your sweetbreads in, stir 'em a little and turn 'em then put in strong Broth and Mushrooms, Pepper and Salt, Cloves and Mace. Let 'em stew half an hour. Put in Forecemeat Balls, Artichoke bottoms cut small and thin. Thicken and serve it with Lemon.

TO COLLER[10] EELLS

Take large Eells and Scour them with salt very well, then slitt them down the back and cutt of their Heads and bone them and stew them well with Salt and pepper and Cloves beaten well and Sifted. Lay large Mace in Rows upon the Eells and a good deal of Shred fennel and some sweet marjoram and Thyme. Strew all these upon the Eells then Roll it up hard and Tye it with pack thread then boyle it with fair water and wine Vinegar and Lemon Pile and a Bundle of sweet herbs, Salt and mace. But first let your liquor boyle then put in your eells. Let it boyle till it be tender then take it up from the Liquor and let it stand till it be cold, then pour your Liquor from the Bones and put in your Eells.

TO MAKE FORCED MEAT BALLS

Take a little Veal and double ye quantity of Suit, sometimes sweet marjoram, Lemon skin all shread very small, bread crumbs beat all together very fine. Make them up with beaten Egg but first season it with pepper and Salt and boyl them quickly in Strong Broth.

TO PREP. HOGS FEET AND EARS YE BEST WAY

When they're nicely Cleaned, put 'em into a Pot with a bay leaf and a large onion, as much water as will cover 'em. Season it with Salt and a little pepper. Bake 'em with Bread. Keep them in this pickle till you want 'em then cut 'em in peices. Fry 'em and for Sause, three spoonfulls of your pickle. Shake in some

Flower and Butter work'd together, a spoonful of Mustard. Lay your ears in ye middle, your feet round 'em, pour your Sause over 'em.

PUDDINGS OF PIGG BLOOD

Take your Blood of a Pigg, sile it thro' a sive. Putt in a Handfull of Salt and abt. a Thimble full of best black pepper, but better, then, half a Quarton of Groats[11] well pickled. While the blood is warm, Stir it well about and let it stand by the fire 3 hours, then carry it into a cool place and let is stand 48 hours. Stir it well once a day. Put in a plate full of Bran, ½ a pound of Ground Rice, a pint of Cream, 5 eggs well beat, 5 or 6 blades of mace, ½ a Nutmeg, 2 or 3 Cloves. Stir all these well together with 3 or 4 pound of Suit well pickled and Shred small then put it into the skins with a handful of Time, a Handfull of Parsley and a sprig or 2 of Sweet marjoram and a small handfull of Sage.

Third Course

TO PRESERVE PEACHES OR APRICOCKS[12] IN BRANDY

Take 8lbs. of Loaf Sugar[13] and make it into a Thick sirrup. Let half of it be put into a Broad Earthen dish or Bason to cool. Then have 50 ripe peaches the down being Rubbed of clean with a piece of Flannel. Have the other ½ Sirrup Scalding hott. Put your Peaches to it and let them boyle gently till they are very tender. Then put them into a Cold Sirrup. Let them be in it till they be thoroughly cold, then take them out again with a Cullender spoon that the Sirrup may drain all from them. Then put in to a quart mouthed pott or jarr and fill it up with Brandy. Lie 'em close down 'neath a Bladder or parchment and let 'em Stand so 24 hours. You pour you're [sic] Brandey from your peaches and boyle it with your two Sirrup till it come to a Candy Height and let it stand till it be cold and put it in your Peaches and keep them Close covered for your use. Apricocks are done the same way only allowing 20 more Apricocks to the same amount of sugar.

TO MAKE LEMON CREAM

Take half a pint of Orange Flower water or Rose water and as much spring water. Pare the Skins from 4 Lemons thin and out the juice from them. Put them together, let it stand and strain into a Skellet.[14] Sweeten it with double refin'd Sugar to your Taste, set it upon a Slow Charchoal fire and keep it with Stirring all one way till it will Jilley, but it must not boyle. Then put it into Glasses or little cups.

TO MAKE MACKROONS

Take your Almonds blanched, beat them but not so small as for Marshpane.[15] In the beating put some rosewater to 'em. Put ½ so much sugar to them as you have Almonds. Take Crumbs of Bread so much as will make it Stiff like paste and pound your Almonds and Bread together. Then take the 4 whites of Eggs and beat them and mingle altogether in a mortar. Then cutt your Wafers and lay a good Spoonfull upon every wafer and make into Shape with your Knife. Then dust some Sugar upon them and lay them upon Sheets of paper and bake them in a Slow Oven.

LONDON WIGGS[16]

Take three pints of Flower, ¼lb of fresh Butter, rub it small in the Flower then take a quarter and a half of Sugar at 8d. per lb. Rub that in as you do Butter, ½ quart'n of Carriway seeds, a little Candid Lemon, 2 Spoonfull of Orange Flower water, 4 whole Eggs, ¼ of a pint of Barm.[17] Mix these with Skim'd milk luke warm. Pull them but do not work them. Set them before the fire to rise. Batter your papers, ¼ of an hour will bake them then Ice them with the white of an Egg and double refin'd Sugar.

BURNT CREAM

Take half a pint of Cream, boyle it with Laurell leaves till it tastes of them, then sweeten it with Loaf Sugar. Take your Yolks of three Eggs, two spoonfulls of Cold Cream and a little more than half spoonfull of Flower. Beat 'em well together then stir them into your hot cream and set over a slow fire Stirring it all yet time so it may not lump. When its thicken'd, put it into a China Dish and grate some Sugar upon it and have ready a hot fire shovel to brown it, to Crisp your Sugar like Candy. Don't Grate on your Sugar till yet moment before ye brown it.

Well, that collection should have cured you of night starvation. If, on the other hand, you decide that an unspecified period of total abstinence from solids and fluids would be the best restorative, then you might recall that you share nothing in common with a certain Lord Langdale. We are indebted to the 18th-century actor, David Garrick, for an insight into His Lordship's epicurean philosophy. Six years before Almary came to Sewerby, Garrick and Lord Langdale were guests of the 3rd Earl of Burlington at his Londesborough estate across the Wolds near Market Weighton. One of Garrick's letters records that, though he himself had such a mixture of ale, champagne, florence (a kind of wine from Florence in Italy), claret and cowslip wine within him, he was not too far gone to notice that My Lord had eaten three plates of soup, two of salmon, one of carp besides the head, two dozen of gudgeons, some eels, with macaroni, omlett *(sic)* and raspberry tart, adding to these, strawberry and cream, pineapple, etc., etc., etc. Garrick then observed that My Lord grew a little sick after the third bottle of burgundy. Spirits were not dampened for long, though, particularly as My Lord then stated seriously that fasting days never agreed with him.

Now read on, for as long as the candle lasts . . .

TO PRESERVE PEACHES IN BRANDY THE FRENCH WAY

To every 50 peaches take 3½lbs of sugar. Make it into a thin Sirrup then take your fruit not full Ripe but near it. Prick them with a Needle and put 'em into your Sirrup which must be Scalting Hott. Keep them under so that the Sirrup may cover all of them. You must not turn them with a Spoon but a bunch of White Feathers – a spoon will break or crack the Skin.

So let them scald for near an hour but not boyle. Then take them of the Fire and with great care Lay one by one into a flatt

Earthon pan glazed and pour your Sirrup over 'em and Let them stand so all Night. The day following, put them again one by one into your preserving pan and then pour the Sirrup. Then set them on the Fire and let 'em have a gentle boyle about ¼ of an hour, then take them with the same care and put them into a glazed Earthen Jarr that has been scalded and dryed before the Fire and rinch'd[18] with Brandy. Put to it 2 Spoonfull of Sirrup and one of Brandy till your Jarr be quite filled up and the fruit well covered. The Sirrup must be a little warm but when cold cover them close with paper and a Bladder at the Top. Your fruit must be fair without Bruises.

TO MAKE RASIN WINE   Given by Mrs. Washington

To every Gall. of water, 6th of Fruit Chopt. Put the water to it Cold, let them stand together 14 Days stirring them every day then press out the Liquor. Put it in your Casks, fill them up every day. Don't bung it up so long as it makes any Noise. When it has stood 2 months, draw it off from the Lees.[19] Wash your casks and put it up again and to about 18 gallons. Put 40% of Iceing Glass[20] disclosed in a little of the wine over the fire stirring it with a stick and Stop it up Close. Let it stand 6 or 8 months then bottle it. If it Shou'd not be fine[21] with the first Drawings of, you must draw it of again and put more fine to it. Smerna[22] Raisins makes ye best wine.

TO MAKE BRANDEY PUNCH

Take 250 oranges, same of Lemons, 200 Jills of Best Brandy, add 12 lbs. of d'ble refined Sugar.

SIRRUP OF VIOLETTS

Take 1lb. of hard Sugar and a pint of water. Boyle it well together and scum it Clean. Then have Ready 6 Ounces of Violetts clean picked and small ground in a bowl. Then put the Sirrup boyling hot to it stirring it well together and strain it thro a Cloth. Bottle it and keep it for your use.

MISS HANNAH HALL METHOD OF BREWING STRONG BEER

To a Hodgshead,[23] 10 Bushels[24] of Malt, 7lb. or 8lb. of Hops to be boyled an Hour or till the Liquor Cracks. Let it stand upon ye Lees 6 or 8 weeks or till its fine. You draw it of and put it into your casks and add a Handfull of Hopps and a quart of Brandy. You lay it up and let it stand a Year. You Bottle it and keep it a Year in the Bottles before you drink it.

February is ye Best time to Brew it in. 7lb. of Hopps, if good, is sufficient. Its better to have it boyle two Hours.

RABBET SAUCE
Parsley and Butter and ye Liver Boyled to be mixed together.

HOW TO MAKE AN O'LEA[25]
Take pidgeons, chickens or Larks – if the former let them be the youngest you can get. You may use all or either of them. If you use Pidgeons, you must force them in the Belley and season them very well with what seasoning you please, or if Convenient, then have ready fry'd sweet ox Pallats,[26] oysters, chestnutts, hard Egg Yolks and Balls of forced meat. Then take a Large Bladder of a Beast, open it and Turn the inside outwards. Season with pepper, Salt Nutmeg and Mace. Then put into the Bladder the aforesaid Ingredients being well seasoned with good seasoning. Mix them as equally together as you can, Tye up your Bladder as close as you can and throw it into a pot of boyling water to boyle. Let it boyle half and hour or ¾, then take it out with a Scimmer for fear of heating and lay it gently in the Driping pan with the knott of the Bladder downwards and do it over with the yolks of Eggs and Drench it over with Grated and minced parsely and let it Lye there to Broyle till you have got the other things ready which must be as follows:
3 chickens cutt in halves, either fry or boyl them. Fry sweet herbs, oysters, Lambs kidneys and Chestnuts roasted. Stew all these together with white wine, 2 Anchovies, Shallots, Shrimps and Capers. Season them to your taste when you stew them. Lay the Ball in the Middle of the dish and all the other things round about it but do not cut open the Bladder till it be at the Table for that will spoil ye Rarity of it. Squeeze on a couple of Oranges, send it up, garnish it with Oranges and what pickle you please.

SYLLABUBS
Take a Quart and ½ a pint of Cream, a pint of Rhenish,[27] ½ a pint of Sack,[28] 3 lemons, 12 Ounces of double refined Sugar and put 'em to the Cream. Grate of the Yellow Rhins and put that in. Squeeze the juice into your wine and put in your Cream, then beat all together with a swisk till Thick enough and fill your Glasses.

ORANGE POPET
Take a Gill of white wine, sweeten it to your taste.
Grate ye Rhind of a Sevel[29] Orange into it. Take a gill and half of

Cream, ye White of an egg well beat then put it into a Glass and cover it. It must be made ye Day before you Use it.

TO MAKE THIN PANCAKES

Take 9 Eggs and a little salt, four Spoonfulls of Flower, a quart of Cream with ½ a lb. of Butter Melted in it. Let it stand till it be Cold, then put it to the Eggs and Flower, Stirring it. Fry them in a dry pan and when they are done enough, turn. Strew some Sugar over them - ½ this Quantity will make a large Dish. Betty always puts them out of the pan upon a flat dish-cover first because she can lay them on more even.

DUTCH SAUCE FOR ALL SORTS OF BOILED FRESH WATER FISH
Lord Staffords Cook

Desolve two Anchoves in a qr. of a pint of Spring Water warm. Take ye yolks of two Eggs, add to them ye Liquor from ye Anchoves Strained thro' a Hair Seive and half a pound of Fresh Butter, together with a Table spoonful of Elder Vinegar. Stir all those over a stove fire with a wisk or a Wooden Spoon ye firmer ye better. Boil it gently untill it's ye Thickness of creame. Then add ye juice of half a Lemon and its finished.

N.B. it must not be made till its Just going to Table and be particularly Careful of stirring all the time or it will curdle.

TO MAKE A RICH PLUMB CAKE
Sister Stanhope

Take eight pound of fine Flower well Dry'd, twelve Pounds of Currants well washed and Pick'd, one pound of fine Sugar beat and sift'd, one ounce of Mace shred small, four pound of Butter, thirty Eggs. Leave out half the whites and beat them very well. Get a quart of Strong Ale yeast, half a pint of Sack, a quart of thick Cream as warm as Milk from the Cow.

Rub the Butter in the Flower and mix all the liquid Things together. Beat your yeast well before you put it in then beat your Cake Well with your hand an hour. Put in the Currants very hot and one pound of Candid Peels in pretty large pieces. Put in the hoop[30] and two hours will bake it.

I only make a fourth part of this quantity.

MINC'D COLLOPS[31]
Sister Shuttleworth

Take Two or three pound of any tender Beef as you would have your Dish of a Size. Cut it as small as you would do Minc'd

Veal. Take an onion, shred it small and fry it a light brown in Butter season'd with Nutmeg, Pepper and Salt, and put it into your pan with your onion and fry it a little whilst it be a light brown. Then put to it a Gill of good Gravey, a spoonful of Wallnut pickle, a little Catchap.[32] Thicken it up with a little Flower and Butter, put it in a little Lemon Juice.

A RECEIPT TO MAKE AN ORANGE PUDDING
Brother Spencer

Take the Outside peal of 3 Sevile Oranges, boyle them in Several Waters till they are Tender, then pound them in a Mortar with 3 quarters of a pound of Sugar. Then blanch and beat, have a pound of Almonds very fine with Orange water to Keep 'em from Oyleing. Then beat 16 Eggs (but 6 Whites only) and a pound of fresh butter together very well untill it is light and hollow. Then put it in a Dish with a Sheet of puff paste at ye bottom and bake it as long as you do Tarts.

GOOSEBERRY WINE
My Mother Greame

To every pound of Gooseberry's pick'd and bruis'd, put a Quart of Water. Let it stand three Days stirring it twice a Day and to every Gall. of Liquor when strain'd of, put three pound of Loaf Sugar. Then put it into a Cask, let it stand half a Year, then Bottle it. If you put a little Brandy into your Cask it will make it better.

TO DRESS A CALVES HEAD TO EAT LIKE TURTLE
My Mother

Lay the Head in water all night to take out the Blood, then boil it just Enough to Bone it. When it is bon'd, season it with Jamaica pepper, a little Mace and Salt. Have ready some forst meat made of a pretty large Lobster boil'd as for eating or some Crowfish.[33] Pick the meat out of the Tails, Clawes and body. Shred it very fine and season it with the above spices and a little Thime and twice as much Parsley both shred very fine. Then mix it up with a Raw Egg and lay it on the Inside of one half of the head and the other half upon it, and tye it with tape to lay round and bake it. Boil your Shells in very strong broth made of any kind of meat and put some of your gravy into the pot when you send it to the oven.

A TASTE OF TINCTURES

It is now, perhaps, providential that by turning Almary's book the other way round, you are confronted with an illuminating amalgam of plagues, palsies, prostrations, pills and potions. It is comforting to know that should you suffer with anything from a sore throat to rabies, there is something here for you.

To Mrs. Greame, Sewerby, near Bridlington,
With Miss Langley's Compliments.   FOR WORMS
A strong decoction[1] of Tansey and Rue, two parts Tansey and one Rue. A coffee cup full is sufficient dose for a grown Person and in less proportion for Children. To be taken two or three times a week in the Morning. It should opperate as gentle Physick. A tea made of Tansey is counted an admirable Stomatick by many people. For the Gout[2] in the Stomach, Take some Tansey, steep it well in Brandy then take the Brandy.

FOR A HEAT IN YE FACE
Take the Juice of Lemon and of common Salt. Take a Soft Cloth and bathe the Heats, and when its at the Worst, wash it with Brandy.

FOR SWELLING IN THE THROAT
Take Salt Petre and Beat it, powder it and mix it with some of the best Brandy, or Take Green Goose Dung and Onyons Roasted. Mix them well together. Put a little Hogs Lard to them. Make 'em hott and Lye it to the Throat. Lye on fresh every 3 or 4 hours till you have Ease.

A RECEIPT FOR DEAFNESS

Take 2 or 3 handfulls of Wormwood,[3] Stamp it and strain it thro' a Cloth. Put the juice into a Turkey Egg Shell, Boyle it upon a slow Fire. Scum with a Tea Spoon while any Scum will rise. Every Night drop 2 or 3 drops of this into your Ear and Lye upon the Contrary side.

FOR BLEEDING AT THE NOSE

Take Hoggs Dung and hold it to your Nose.

A CERTAIN CURE FOR THE BITE OF A MAD DOG

Let the Patient be blooded[4] at the arm. 9 or 10 oz. of the Herb called in Lattain *Lichen cineritius*, in English Ash Coloured Ground Liverwort, clean, dryed and powdered. Half an oz. of Black pepper powdered. Mix them well together and divide the powder into 4 Doses, one of which must be taken every morning, Fasting for 4 mornings successively, in half a pint of Cows milk warm. After these, 4 Cloves are taken. The patient must go into a Cold Bathe or a Cold spring or River every morning fasting for a month. He must be dipt all over but not stay in with his head above water Longer than half a minute. If the water be very Cold he must go in three Times a week for 14 nights Longer.
NB. the Lichen is a very common herb and Grows commonly in a Sandy and Barren soil all over England. The right time to gather it is in ye Months October or Novr.

LADY WENTWORTH'S CORDIAL

Take a Jill of cynamond *Aqua marabilis*,[5] ½ a Gill of Lady Allen's Water,[6] 1 Gill of Black Cherry Water, 1 Gill of Mint Water, ¼ oz. of pearl[7] prepared. Mix all those well together, sweeten them to your Taste with Sirrup of Clove, Gilliflowers. If it be stronger than you Like it, you may put in more Black Cherrey water. You may take a spoonful when and as often as you please. *Probatum Est.*[8]

FOR THE WIND COLLIC

Take a spoonful of Brandy and mix of new milk. Mingle them and drink of it. Lye down on the Bed and keep yourself warm.

A REMEDY GOOD FOR AN INWARD PAIN

Take 1lb. of Horse Dung, ½lb. of green venus Treackle, 2 handfull of Camomile Flowers. Let it all be steeped in New Milk and distilled upon a cold sill.

FOR THE WORMS

Take as much of the powder of Salprunella[9] as will Lye on a 6d,[10] three mornings together, in liquid. Let them rest 3 mornings more.

FOR THE AGUE

Twenty grains of Allum,[11] Ten of Nutmeg – to be given an Hour before the fit comes on. To have three fits before you take this medicin.

VIPER BROTH   Dr. Cookson

Take one viper, cut of the head, skin it, cut it into pieces. One Chicken skinned or a pound of Mutton clean picked from fat, one quart of water boiled to one pint and a half which strain for use.

EYE WATER   Mrs. Raystrick

White vitriol[12] two Drams, Rose water one Pint, well shaken together with which Wash your Eyes at pleasure.

EYE WATER   My Mother

Take a piece of white Vitriol the size of a good large Nut Meg, pour a large Basin of boiling Water upon it. Let it stand whilst it's Cold then clean it of and put it in Bottles.

NB: This is good for an Eye that has a rheum[13] but not a dry Eye.

FOR STIFF AND WEAK KNEES   Miss Langley

Knuckle Oil to be got at the Butchers to be applyed three or four times a day.

FOR A CONTRACTION IN THE SINEWS   Miss Langley

Beat one Egg well in a spoonfull of water, rub the part two or three times a Day with it. This has done great cures.

FOR THE JAUNDICE Miss Langley

Take half a pint of Mountain wine or sack, half a jill of sheep Dung, four pennyworth of saffron. Let it stand several hours and take two spoonfulls night and morning.

FOR THE STING OF A BEE OR WASP

Take a Slice of Onion, put a little Salt upon it, apply it to the part affected and keep it on twenty minutes or half an hour. If applyed Immediately it will prevent it swelling and Speedily remove the pain. If you wett the place a little before you lay it on, it will take Effect the sooner.

FOR THE RHEUMATISM
From the Annual Register vol. 9 page 167
Take a Garlick, two cloves, gum ammoniac[14] one drach'm.[15] Blend them into two or three Colusses[16] with fair water and swallow them one at night and one in the morning. Drink, while taking this recipe, Sassafras[17] tea made very strong so as to have the tea pot fill'd with chips. This is generally found to banish the rheumatism and even contractions of the joints in a few times taking. It is very famous in America.

FOR THE GRIPES IN YOUNG CHILDREN
Five grains of Magnetia[18] and three of Rhubarb or one drop or two drops of Hartshorn[19] have been of great service in this Complaint.

A RECIPE FOR BURNT OINTMENT
Take of Houseleck,[20] smooth plantin and the young stalks and leaves of Dwarf elder of each one a pound. Cut and stamp them very much, then put to them a quarter of a pint of vinegar and three or four spoonfulls of Urine. Stamp them well together then put to them four ounces of old tallow candles and three pints of hogs lard rendered and melted. Boyle all these together two hours, stirring them, then strain it through a Canvas and set it on the fire again and put to it half a pound of Bees wax slic'd.
Let it boyle a quarter of an hour then strain it again and put it into a pot and when it is cold, take of all the green part till you come at a blackish sediment which sediment is of no use.
The other part which was taken of you must just melt and pour into pots for use. Rub fine cap Paper till it is very soft then spread the Ointment very thin over it and having first anointed the burn with the ointment method and lay on the paper to cover it. Spread with the Ointment three times a day till quite healed and use nothing else for inflamed ulcers, Emerods,[21] piles, and for womens niples if not cancer'd, being laid on a alewort leaf. If the liver be hot, anoint that part of the breast with it. It also cures scabby Hands.

FOR MR. GREAME   June 24th, 1758
When the Gout is in ye Head or Stomach, Scrape three or four Roots of Horseradish into half a pale of Hot Water. Put in your Feet and keep it Cover'd Close.

FOR THE GOUT OR CHOLICK[22]

1¼ pnd of Raisins ston'd, Chop'd. ½ an Ounce Fennel Seed.
¼ pnd of Rhubarb – thin slic'd. ¼ an Ounce Saffron
1 Ounce of Sena   ¼ of an Ounce Liquorice
½ an Ounce Corriander Seed   ¼ of an Ounce Cocheneal
Brandy – one Gallon

Infuse all these in a Large Stone Bottle for ten Days, shaking the Bottle Daily, then Strain it of. You may add to your Remaining Ingredients five pints of Brandy and when it has stood Six Weeks it will be, when strain'd, as good as the first. In extream great Pain at the Stomach, you may take a Wine Glass full. It sometimes Operates both way's. It is likewise good for any thing that lyes heavy at the Stomach to remove it.

AN INFALLIBLE RECEIPT FOR THE BITES OF A MAD DOG

Take one Ounce of the best Dragon's blood,[23] of Spanish Brown[24] one ounce and a half, of box leaves dried, pounded and sifted through a fine Sieve five ounces. Mix these together and take it in the following manner:

To a Man or a Woman, in the Morning, fasting, one large tablespoonful in a little gruel, white wine, Whey or warm ale.
To children, a quantity in proportion to their age. Observe to refrian from any food for three hours after taking.
To a horse or cow, two spoonfuls in warme water or mixed in butter.
To a hog, one spoonful and a half.
To a dog, a Spoonful.
The above medicine should be taken by each three mornings successively as soon after bit as possible.

This Receipt taken out of the Gentleman's London Monthly Magazine for March, 1764 . . .

By now your eyes are heavy and your candle is beginning to gutter. Soon, the servants will be astir. So many intriguing headings remain: Black Pills, White Plaister, Green Salve, Purple Dye, Yellow Water; For Scurvey in the Gums and Pimples on the Face. You have always wanted an efficacious remedy for the Hoop and a Cordial for a Child in Vomiting; if you had only brought down your own folio you could have transcribed the Calve's Lung Water for Hektic Consumption and the mysteries of Lady Allen's Water.

Be that as it may, there is always tomorrow night.

A DIGESTIF

When John Greame the Younger died in 1798, aged 89, history repeated itself; as Almary's and John Spencer's nephew, Walter Spencer-Stanhope, had inherited Cannon Hall on his Uncle's death in 1775, so Almary's husband's nephew inherited Sewerby. At the age of 38, John Greame the Even Younger brought his second wife Elizabeth to be Mistress of the House, not the easiest of roles as Almary remained in residence. She had been left the house, its contents and lands to enjoy for her lifetime, including a coach and eight horses. Here occurred another of history's action replays, for she herself had arrived at Sewerby while her husband's mother was still resident. But common sense was one of Almary's qualities, which, coupled with her philosophical approach to life, ensured that there was a seamless continuation from her generation to the next.

Judging by the alterations to the property John made round his aunt, the two of them must have been on amicable enough terms, for he clamped a pair of two-storied, bow-fronted wings onto the west and east sides of the old house, like a couple of squat book ends and painted out the red brickwork with a neutral stone colour more in keeping with early Regency taste and cheaper than stucco. He added the semi-circular Doric portico to enhance the undulating bow effect to the earlier severity, and redesigned the doorcase, blocking up his Grandfather's fanlight.

The latest dateable entry in Almary's book is on a loose piece of paper watermarked 1811 – a recipe for 20 gallons of Black Currant Wine requiring 10 stone of currants.

Almary survived the alterations and establishment of the new family in her old home, dying at the same age as her husband in 1812, the year that saw *Comet*, the first steamship, sail down the river Clyde, and the birth of Charles Dickens.

Successive generations inhabited Sewerby House, each contributing its own mark in the developing tides of time and seamarks flushing man and his fortunes along. But by 1934 the family had sold up to the then Bridlington Corporation. Before its official opening as a Public Amenity by Amy Johnson, on 1 June 1936, a public auction was held to dispose of the superfluous contents and household effects.

The editor's father, Maurice Horspool, dramatist and broadcaster, came away with the Housekeeping Book, fascinated as much by its historical associations as its literary charms and curiosities. He used it as the basis for 4 articles in his regular column for the *Bridlington Free Press* in July 1935. Though it became one of his most treasured possessions, he was unaware that it was anything more than a book typical of its day. It was only after it had passed into the present editor's eager hands that, having seen an example of Almary's handwriting, he recognised the same hand at work amongst its yellowing pages.

Maurice's friend, Francis Johnson, the distinguished architect and lecturer, was able to purchase, at the same sale, four of Almary's 12 dining chairs in the Chippendale style, and the lacquer longcase clock, amongst other items.

Between these two enthusiasts, whose friendship had begun at Bridlington School, where Maurice's father, Robert Horspool, was Art Master, the book and the chairs are linked to represent a fundamental social area: the sense of well-being engendered by food, drink and conviviality – some of the more pleasurable aspects of man's rocky existence. The possession of a manuscript from an age distant from ours yet strangely relevant, creates an immediate ability to touch time and, like savouring a good wine, to roll it reflectively about the palate of the mind, and imagine.

Recipe books, like fashions, come and go; all her married life the editor's mother kept adding assiduously to the one she began in the early 1930s. It ended up as fat as the Christmas goose Scrooge bought for the Cratchit family.

Each generation and each fashion adds a further pinch of seasoning to an ever richer bill of fare.

FIN

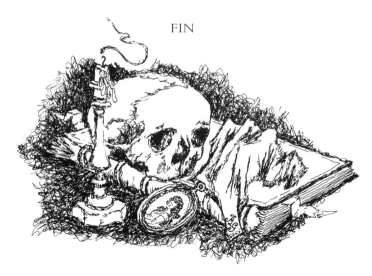

Appendix I

In the editor's possession is a quarto (23cm x 15cm) pack of pages stitched together, entitled *The London Magazine or Gentleman's Monthly Intelligencer,* for April 1759. It is the kind of improving publication Almary and other ladies, wishing to be kept informed, would have been pleased to have access to, even though it was directed more to the male market. Its title page displays a charmingly naïve engraving of Old London Bridge and the City bristling with Wren steeples, above a list of the month's contents. On page 205 is to be found *WINE useful in some Sorts of FEVERS.* This article is constrained between a history of the last session of Parliament, mathematical questions and solutions, a review of births, marriages, promotions, bankrupts and deaths, and the musical notation of an 18-bar country dance in G major under the promising heading *Commodore Howe's Ramble:*

> In feverish Disorders, even the most moderate Use of Wine has generally been thought to be pernicious, and yet in some Sorts of Fevers, it is not only salutary but necessary, as it appears from Dr. Home's *Medical Facts and Experiments,* lately published, who, in his Treatise on the Pulse, writes thus:
>
> A Gentleman, after a day's journey, had a quick, weak pulse, and a general uneasiness; these complaints seeming to come from fatigue and weakness, he was advised to drink some glasses of wine; his pulse immediately turned calm after that.
>
> A lady, in the latter end of a hectick fever when her pulse was very quick and very weak, took some wine; immediately after this her pulse turned calm.
>
> A gentleman in the hectick fever of old age, who had lived very temperately for many years, was advised by me to begin the regular use of wine. A quarter of an hour after his first dose, his pulse was fuller, and 18 beats in a minute slower than when he got it. It always had a similar effect on him.
>
> I have oftentimes seen effects similar to these, upon giving wine in low fevers. It is but lately since physicians measured the velocity of the pulse with that accuracy that they do now.
>
> But whence is it, or in what state of the body happens it, that wine produces an effect so very different from its general tendency? There are always, in these

cases, a general debility, with a weak, soft pulse, which argues a weakness in the motion of the heart and arteries. These not being able to protrude (*sic*) the usual quantity of blood, must make up, for want of strength, by repeating their contractions oftener, and raising a degree of fever. Wine, which encreases the strength of these motive powers, must diminish a fever which arises from their weakness.

At the end of April's edition, under the cryptic caption B-K-R-TS, as if the word Bankrupts should barely be whispered for shame, is listed 15 names in minute, dispirited print, amongst whom is Richard Scott, a carpenter of Mayton (Myton) in Kingston Upon Hull.

Under DEATHS, in loud, chunky letters like the man himself, is to be found, for 14 April, George Frederick Handel, Esq., the celebrated musician, aged 77 (he was 74). The blind old man of Brook Street, Mayfair, had been renowned in his heyday for his love of food and hearty (some said gross) appetite.

It would be interesting to know the eating and drinking habits of the aptly named Mrs. Savory, of Old Palace Yard, who had died 11 days earlier, aged 104. On the 15th, Mary Hall, of Bishophill the Elder, in York, died aged 105. Almary, three years into her life at Sewerby, would have relished intelligence such as this over her tea table, before passing on to her spinet in anticipation of an agreeable ramble, in a major key, with Commodore Howe.

Appendix II

THE REGENT'S OR GEORGE IV'S PUNCH

Pare as thin as possible the rinds of two China oranges, of two lemons and of one Seville orange, and infuse them for an hour in half a pint of cold thin syrup; then add to them the juice of the fruit.

Make a pint of strong green tea, sweeten it well with fine sugar, and when it is quite cold, add to it the fruit and syrup, with a glass of the best old Jamaica rum, a glass of brandy, one of arrack,★ one of pineapple syrup, and two bottles of Champagne; pass the whole through a fine lawn sieve until it is perfectly clear, then bottle and put it into ice until dinner is served.

Eliza Acton. Modern Cookery, 1845.

★a term used in India to designate any type of spirituous liquor, especially that distilled from coconut, rice or sugar cane.

Appendix III

Glossary of terms found in the recipes.

1. SAVOURY BALLS – forcemeat: a mixture of chopped or minced ingredients used for stuffing; forcemeat balls.
2. PILE – peel.
3. ALEGAR – sour ale and made from ale.
4. KETTLE – fish kettle: a long-lidded container for poaching Salmon, etc.
5. SMELTS – small delicate fishes; also used as a garnish.
6. SALTS PEETER – saltpetre: potassium nitrate, a colourless crystalline compound used as a food preservative, especially for curing ham, bacon, etc.
7. ROACH ALLUM – a salt extract from a member of the fresh water carp family.
8. BARBERRIES – *burberis vulgaris:* an acid fruit similar to the tamarind.
9. CAWDLE – caudle: a warm spiced invalid drink made with wine and oats like a thin gruel.
10. COLLER – collar: to roll up and bind with twine and string.
11. GROATS – the crushed and huskless grains of oats and other cereals; also parts of the oat kernel.
12. APRICOCKS – apricots.
13. LOAF SUGAR – sugar bought in tall cones called 'loaves;' pieces were broken off for use with sugar nippers.
14. SKILLET – a small metal vessel with three feet and long handle for boiling water and syrups.
15. MARSHPANE – also MARCHPANE: marzipan – almond paste.
16. WIGGS – wig: a type of cake containing caraway seeds rather like a scone.
17. BARM – yeasty froth on fermenting malt liquors.
18. RINCH'D – rinsed.
19. LEES – sediment.
20. ICEINGLASS – isinglass: gelatine made from air bladders of fresh water fish and used as a clarifying agent.
21. FINE – clear.

22   SMERNA – Smyrna: a coastal town then in Greece; renamed Izmir since 1922, it now belongs to Turkey.

23   HOGSHEAD – a unit of capacity for alcoholic drinks or a large cask for transporting wines and spirits (see Appendix V).

24   BUSHEL – dry measure containing eight gallons.

25   O'LEA – a type of haggis: made from sheep's or calves offal, oatmeal, suet and seasonings boiled in a skin made from the animal's stomach. Popular in Scotland.

26   PALLATS – probably palates (roof of the mouth) also ox tongue.

27   RHENISH – an imported Rhine wine, dry and white, now known as hock.

28   SACK – dry white wine imported from south-west Europe.

29   SEVEL – Seville, in Spain.

30   HOOP – cake tin for baking the mixture in.

31   COLLOPS – small slices of fleshy lumps of meat or generally anything.

32   CATCHAP – ketchup: any of various piquant sauces containing vinegar.

33   CROWFISH – crayfish: any freshwater crustacean resembling a small lobster.

Appendix IV

Glossary of terms found in the pharmacopoeia.

1   DECOCTION- extraction of water soluble substances by boiling.

2   GOUT – painful inflammation in certain joints, especially the foot and big toe.

3   WORMWOOD - *Artemisia absinthium:* European plant yielding a bitter extract; often used for acidic stomach and as an aid to digestion and general health. One of the main ingredients of the addictive alcoholic drink absinthe, technically a gin and a potent green in colour.

4   BLOODED - to be bled; blood-letting by opening an arm vein with a lancet. Believed to lessen the presence of red corpuscles and thus reduce fevers, at the same time relieving pressure on the heart and brain.

5   CYNAMOND *AQUA MIRABILIS*- 'Wonderful Cinnamon Water' for the relief of stomach cramps and looseness.

6   LADY ALLEN'S WATER - an infusion of herbs, liquorice root and white wine for the stomach and bowels.

7   PEARL - pearl-barley: the seed of common barley ground into small pear-like grains.

8   *PROBATUM EST* - Latin: 'It is Proved.' An expression often added to the receipt for the cure of a disease or complaint denoting that it has been proved successful.

9   SALPRUNELLA - Sal-Prunella: another name for saltpetre.

10   6d – sixpence: - a small silver coin worth six old pence.

11   ALLUM - alum: a mineral salt.

12   WHITE VITRIOL - zinc sulphate: diluted vitriolic acid for indigestion and intestinal complaints.

13   RHEUM - a watery discharge.

14   GUM AMMONIAC - the juice of the Persian plant *Dorema ammoniacum,* rich in ammonia salts.

15   DRACH'M - drachm: a measure of weight (see Appendix V).

16   COLUSSES - callous: in a state of hardness or hardnesses; i.e. tablets, pills, etc.

17   SASSAFRAS - *Sassafras albidium:* North American aromatic dried root bark of the laurel family. Good for indigestion and wind.

18   MAGNETIA - magnesia: magnesium oxide. Usually mixed with chalk; neutralises stomach acids and acts as a mild purgative.

19   HARTSHORN - the horn of the hart or male deer. An impure solution of carbonate of ammonia when grated and distilled. Also used to make a jelly similar to calvesfoot: in paste form, used as a cleaner for silver plate. Recommended by Mrs. Beeton (entry 2316) 1861.

20   HOUSELECK - houseleek; *Sempervivium tectorum:* also called hen-and-chickens; succulent herbal plant long believed effective in relieving inflammation and swelling.

21   EMERODS - haemorrhoids.

22   CHOLIC - colic: spasmodic abdominal pains and inflammation.

23   DRAGON'S BLOOD - bright red resinous gum from the palm fruit.

24   SPANISH BROWN - a species of earth, containing iron, usually used in paints.

Appendix V

Archaic weights and measures
some of which are referred to
in the text.

Dry Weights

Imperial		*Approx. metric equivalent*
20 grains	= 1 scruple	–
3 scruples	= 1 drachm	–
8 drachms	= 1 ounce (oz.)	28g
16 ounces	= 1 pound (lb.)	450g
14 pounds	= 1 stone	6.35kg
2 stone	= 1 quarter	12.7kg
4 quarters	= 1 hundredweight	50.8kg
20 hundredweights	= 1 ton	1016kg

Wet Measures

Imperial		*Approx. metric equivalent*
1 gill/jill	= ¼ of a pint	100-125 ml
1 pint	= ⅛ of a gallon	575-600 ml
2 pints	= 1 quart	1.14 litres
4 quarts	= 1 gallon	4.56 litres

hogshead: approximately 50 gallons (228 litres)
pipe: approximately 2 hogsheads (roughly 480 bottles)
bushel: a dry measure of approximately 8 gallons (36.48 litres)
peck: a quarter of a bushel – a dry measure of 8 quarts

Bibliography

Beeton, I., *The Book of Household Management, 1861* (1982).
Brown, P., *Pyramids of Pleasure: Eating and Drinking in the 18th Century*. (York, 1990).
Hampson, J., *The English at Table*. (1946).
Johnson, F., *Sewerby House and Park*. (Bridlington, 1947).
Neave, D., *Londesborough: History of an Estate Village*. (Driffield, 1994).
Ogilvie, J., *The Comprehensive English Dictionary*. (1877).
Owen, H., *Stanhope, Atkinson, Haddon and Shaw: Four North Country Families* (1985).
Pullar, P., *Consuming Passions: A History of English Food and Appetite*. (1970).
Reece, R., *The Medical Guide*. (1814).
Woodward, M., *John Gerarde's Herball or General Historie of Plantes, 1597*. (1964).

Further Reading

Elek, P. and E., *Coaching Days of England* (1966).
Fletcher, R., *The Parkers at Saltram* (1970).
Girouard, M., *Life in the English Country House* (1978).
Girouard, M., *A Country House Companion* (Leicester, 1992).
Hardyment, C., (Ed). *The Housekeeping Book of Susannah Whatman* (1988).
Horspool, R. D., *The House of Powolny: Life and Death of a Hull Restaurant* (Beverley, 2000).
Jekyll, G, and Jones, S., *Old English Household Life* (1945).
Paston-Williams, S., *A Book of Historical Recipes*. (1995).